Dear Warrior:

Thank you for purchasing the Teaching Warrior: 14 Day Journal Guide. I am excited to be a pathfinder for you and to help you turn the corners of life. I hope that you find this journal useful, friendly, and inspiring.

Journaling is important to developing and crafting your voice. I learned how to journal in middle school. As I reflect on my collections of journals, I am always amazed at all of the different people, spaces, and places that have informed my personal and professional growth. It helps to safely look back at my struggles and to celebrate my accomplishments and those dear to me.

There are times that I feel like my journaling is more of a list of the activities from the day—and in that moment, I choose not to judge myself. I accept and respect the process.

If you have never journaled before, I want to ask you to start with protecting the quiet. Make time each day—to be honest it doesn't have to be the same time each day because we have to always make adjustments. Be open and honest with your reflections and trust the process.

If you'd like a little boost to get started, check out my show on YouTube by searching The Dr. Selma B. Show. You'll see how I integrate journaling with short confidence-boosting videos to advocate for you.

As an educator, I advocate for different learning styles. A journal doesn't have to be in writing. The questions in this journal offer a structure. If you feel like you are not ready to write every day or weekly, then I encourage you to use a voice recorder or complete a video journal to answer the questions. What matters most is that you engage in the journaling process. Trust ... and you will hone your voice.

The pages of our day seem to always be always filled. A blank page gives you your power back and allows you to claim your breakthrough. You can do this! You can write caring, open, and meaningful reflections. I hope you'll complete this guide and have it as a product that you can constantly refer to. Beloved ... use it until it becomes dog-eared and stained with your hopes.

Dream Big and Have Fun!

Dr. Selma K. Bartholomew
Dr. Selma K. Bartholomew "Dr. B."
President
PartnerWithLegacy

The Powerful Impact of Journaling

Teaching changes lives. It is not a spectator sport. I learned that what I do makes a difference when I taught physics at Jacqueline Kennedy Onassis High School in NYC. In my first semester teaching, I had a young black male student named Jason. He—like so many of my students—did not love science and couldn't see the value of it. I struggled with keeping him and much of the rest of the class engaged. I needed help.

My science team colleagues came to my classroom to observe my lessons and then gave me the tools I needed to continue. I put a notebook structure in place and re-organized my goals to include a project for every unit. As their first project, my students were charged with creating a model of our solar system. In addition, the students had to write in a dedicated journal notebook once a week to share their feelings about their first year in high school, create a story, or write about any topic they wanted to share. They just needed to write something in their journals about their journey.

Jason wrote the most wonderful stories about the trips he would take to the moon with his dad. I was instantly intrigued with what he shared in his journal entries.

In the spring parent teacher conference night, I met his Mom. I had my pre-planned speech: I would tell her what we are doing in the class. Then, I would share their child's grade. Finally, I would add that "yes" he is a pleasure to teach.

After I did my "speech," Jason's mother reached into her bag and pulled out a letter. The top of the letter contained a colored pencil drawing of the stars and all of the planets. The details were extraordinary. But … I didn't understand. Why is she showing me a letter? She shared with me that Jason's father was in prison and he had not seen his son in more than two years. However, this year he and Jason agreed to start corresponding in writing.

When his dad learned that Jason was doing a project every month for science, he decided to encourage him. His father would not only write to Jason but visit the prison library and research and learn about the science topic for himself. And every letter included a beautiful drawing—gorgeous storytelling that reflected what Jason was learning for our science project. I found myself in tears.

Teaching Matters.

How to Use the Teaching Warrior: 14 Day Journal Guide Crafting the Inner Warrior Within

Watch The Dr. Selma B. Show Stop Doing and Start Achieving

Make time to reflect and complete your journal.

Practice being openminded and put the words in your heart on the pages.

You may also record your answers to the journal questions.

You may also complete a video journal. What matters is working through the process of reflecting.

> *May you enjoy the simple gifts of each season in your life, cherish each peaceful moment. Journaling is a reminder of life's sweet joys, the beauty and the love of family and friends. Let's get Started!*
> *—Dr. B.*

Teaching Warrior: Journal Guide

Day 1

What moment or event called you to the teaching profession? What inspired you to be a teacher? What will be your legacy?

Teaching Warrior: Journal Guide

Day 2

Teaching is a profession that is both an art and a science. As an educator every domain and act of our profession is to inspire change, develop voice, and confidence. To become a master teacher, you must continuously challenge yourself to identify ways to engage with our learners. What will you do to ensure learners become active participants in the learning process?

Teaching Warrior: Journal Guide

Day 3

What are your beliefs about learning? Do you believe anyone can learn? How will you rise above environmental and societal challenges and send a message to learners that you believe in their potential?

Teaching Warrior: Journal Guide

~

Day 4

To become a successful educator, it is imperative that we know our students as individuals. What will you do to get to know your individual student's strengths, interests and academic goals?

Teaching Warrior: Journal Guide

Day 5

The classroom should never be a boring place and that is why your pedagogy matters. It is also important to note that an exciting classroom is not always an academically rigorous classroom. You must create that environment where excitement coexist with academic rigor. What will you do differently to disrupt patterns? Who will you ask for help?

Teaching Warrior: Journal Guide

Day 6

Teachers are not rescue pilots—our children do not need saving. Are you grounding your pedagogy in pity or love? What is a pedagogy rooted in care and love look like, feel like and sound like? What are the benefits for you as the teacher? Benefits for the students? Benefits for community? Benefits for our world?

Teaching Warrior: Journal Guide

Day 7

What are your beliefs about parent engagement? Are their spaces and opportunities for parents (and those in a child's "Network of Care") to foster a strong learning culture? Are you telling what your 'subject' is about rather than engaging around 'goals' for learning and the habits of mind you are seeking to develop?

Teaching Warrior: Journal Guide

Day 8

You must practice what you teach. How will you promote your wellness and engage in an ongoing process of improving your mind, body, and soul? What is one small step you can take today?

Teaching Warrior: Journal Guide

~

Day 9

Your classroom should never be your kingdom or island. Are you aware of when you are exercising power in your classroom? How do you feel about letting go of the power and control?

Teaching Warrior: Journal Guide

Day 10

Describe your commitment to cultural diversity? What will you be patient and diligent about learning? Are you aware of social and political movements and how they have shaped the teaching profession? Being open to diversity also means welcoming dissent. Where in your practice do you engage with ideas that oppose from your closely held beliefs?

Teaching Warrior: Journal Guide

Day 11

Without question, most of us learned from schools and were taught in classrooms that did not validate diversity. Reflect closely and you will see that the experience is true for teachers of all backgrounds. As a result, the goals of getting to a culturally relevant pedagogy and multicultural education is challenging. It may look like an unwillingness, but in reality it is rooted in fear of not knowing how to approach teaching from a standpoint of having to address awareness of diversity. We all have fears about being judged. How do you conceptualize learning? What does passive versus active learning look like? Feel like? Sound like?

Teaching Warrior: Journal Guide

Day 12

What is the nature of the relationship you are seeking to build with your students? How will you nurture and grow that relationship?

Teaching Warrior: Journal Guide

Day 13

Every day you wake up and take breath into your lungs is a second chance. Do you believe in second chances in your classroom? How will you let your students know your expectations? How will you create a culture of love and second chances?

Teaching Warrior: Journal Guide

Day 14

Metaphors help us makes sense of big ideas. My metaphor for teaching is that teaching is not a spectator sport. You have to put in the work to achieve. What is your metaphor for your practice?

Teaching Warrior: Journal Guide

Day 15

The gap between theory and practice in education is what causes students to fall between the cracks and behind. What are the theories that inform your practice?

Teaching Warrior: Journal Guide

Day 16

Are you stuck in a rut? Go ahead and smile, take a breath—we have all been there as teachers, however we can move on from it and let it go. What do you think the difference is between lecturing and facilitating? Are you seeking to only impact your students intellectually? Do you truly believe that you have the power to impact the whole child? And how students perceive and know themselves beyond the classroom and school building?

Teaching Warrior: Journal Guide

Day 17

As a teacher, I am grateful for...

Teaching Warrior: Journal Guide

Day 18

In the end, it is the teacher's voice that all students enter the classroom ready to listen to. Our voice as teachers must help our students learn how to listen, how to listen to their soul, how to listen to their peers and most importantly how to 'hear' one another and pay attention their inner spirit. What are your students 'hearing' from your voice?

Teacher Warrior: Stop Doing and Start Achieving

Strategic, Measurable, Attainable, Realistic, and Timely (SMART) Goals.
What are you seeking to achieve?

Priorities: What must you focus on to get to your goals?
   1. _____
   2. _____
   3. _____
   4. _____
   5. _____

To Do List: Handling the small things once will help you gain and keep your momentum. You will be amazed at how quickly you get to your goals and priorities.
   1. _____
   2. _____
   3. _____
   4. _____
   5. _____

Teacher Warrior: Stop Doing and Start Achieving

Strategic, Measurable, Attainable, Realistic, and Timely (SMART) Goals.
What are you seeking to achieve?

Priorities: What must you focus on to get to your goals?
1. _____
2. _____
3. _____
4. _____
5. _____

To Do List: Handling the small things once will help you gain and keep your momentum. You will be amazed at how quickly you get to your goals and priorities.
1. _____
2. _____
3. _____
4. _____
5. _____

Teacher Warrior: Stop Doing and Start Achieving

Strategic, Measurable, Attainable, Realistic, and Timely (SMART) Goals.
What are you seeking to achieve?

Priorities: What must you focus on to get to your goals?
1. _____
2. _____
3. _____
4. _____
5. _____

To Do List: Handling the small things once will help you gain and keep your momentum. You will be amazed at how quickly you get to your goals and priorities.
1. _____
2. _____
3. _____
4. _____
5. _____

Teacher Warrior: Stop Doing and Start Achieving

Strategic, Measurable, Attainable, Realistic, and Timely (SMART) Goals.
What are you seeking to achieve?

Priorities: What must you focus on to get to your goals?
1. _____
2. _____
3. _____
4. _____
5. _____

To Do List: Handling the small things once will help you gain and keep your momentum. You will be amazed at how quickly you get to your goals and priorities.
1. _____
2. _____
3. _____
4. _____
5. _____

Teacher Warrior: Stop Doing and Start Achieving

Strategic, Measurable, Attainable, Realistic, and Timely (SMART) Goals.
What are you seeking to achieve?

Priorities: What must you focus on to get to your goals?
1. _____
2. _____
3. _____
4. _____
5. _____

To Do List: Handling the small things once will help you gain and keep your momentum. You will be amazed at how quickly you get to your goals and priorities.
1. _____
2. _____
3. _____
4. _____
5. _____

Teacher Warrior: Stop Doing and Start Achieving

Strategic, Measurable, Attainable, Realistic, and Timely (SMART) Goals.
What are you seeking to achieve?

Priorities: What must you focus on to get to your goals?
1. _____
2. _____
3. _____
4. _____
5. _____

To Do List: Handling the small things once will help you gain and keep your momentum. You will be amazed at how quickly you get to your goals and priorities.
1. _____
2. _____
3. _____
4. _____
5. _____

Teacher Warrior: Stop Doing and Start Achieving

Strategic, Measurable, Attainable, Realistic, and Timely (SMART) Goals.
What are you seeking to achieve?

Priorities: What must you focus on to get to your goals?
1. _____
2. _____
3. _____
4. _____
5. _____

To Do List: Handling the small things once will help you gain and keep your momentum. You will be amazed at how quickly you get to your goals and priorities.
1. _____
2. _____
3. _____
4. _____
5. _____

Teacher Warrior: Stop Doing and Start Achieving

Strategic, Measurable, Attainable, Realistic, and Timely (SMART) Goals.
What are you seeking to achieve?

Priorities: What must you focus on to get to your goals?
1. _____
2. _____
3. _____
4. _____
5. _____

To Do List: Handling the small things once will help you gain and keep your momentum. You will be amazed at how quickly you get to your goals and priorities.
1. _____
2. _____
3. _____
4. _____
5. _____

Continue to Craft the Inner Warrior Within.

Check Out Our Warrior Journal Series Available on Amazon

Get Inspired

Join Our Community of Warriors. Subscribe Today and Get for Free Our

Inspiration Warrior:
Introduction Journal Guide

PartnerWithLegacy
Home of

THE
DR. SELMA B
Show

About The Author

Dr. Selma K. Bartholomew, known as Dr. B., for more than 25 years, has worked to improve educational outcomes for children and families. She began her career teaching mathematics at Lehman College in the Bronx, taught math and physics at Jacqueline Kennedy Onassis High School in NY, students in group homes, women in prison, and in Fordham University's Graduate School of Education. In 2008, she stepped out on faith and founded her company PartnerWithLegacy to help schools become a place of purpose, passion, and innovation. PartnerWithLegacy's work in STEM is transformative and rests on the theory of learning that Math is a Language.

Dr. B's love for journaling and writing was cultivated growing up in Harlem and spending hours after school getting lost in books at the famous Countee Cullen and Arturo Schomburg Library. Her goal is to inspire and motivate writers and readers (of ALL ages) to find their voice and fight for their passion. Connect with her to learn more about the work of her company, team and mission. Get inspired by visiting PartnerWithLegacy's YouTube channel—Home of The Dr. Selma B. Show.